Technology in the
Battle of Britain

Written by Nick Hunter

Contents

Collins

D0227158

Their finest hour

In September 1939, Europe
was plunged into war.
Great Britain and France
declared war on Nazi
Germany after German
leader Adolf Hitler's
forces invaded Poland.
Germany launched
a series of devastating
attacks in April and
May 1940. In a few weeks,
German forces overran Denmark,
Norway, the Netherlands, Belgium and finally France.
Would Britain be invaded next?

Winston Churchill, 1940

In May, Britain and France managed to **evacuate**
340,000 soldiers from the beaches of Dunkirk, northern France.
But this heroic rescue couldn't hide the fact that the **Allies** had
no answer to Germany's fast-moving military machine.

British Prime Minister Winston Churchill made a speech on 18th
June to rally support for the fight against Germany. He said that
future generations would see this battle as "their finest hour".

Churchill knew that it would take more than bravery to save Britain. Victory in the Battle of Britain would depend on the latest military technology. Engineers and scientists would be just as important as fighter pilots and soldiers.

The threat of bombing raids made Britain's cities very dangerous. Many children were evacuated to live in the country.

Battle lines drawn

In July 1940, Hitler ordered commanders to draw up plans for invasion of Britain. Germany's staggering military successes had all been achieved on land, with the German air force, called the Luftwaffe, supporting the army.

To invade Britain, Germany would have to attack across the English Channel. No one had launched a successful invasion of Britain since William the Conqueror in 1066.

Hitler's "**Blitzkrieg**", or "lightning war", **tactics** used tanks and foot soldiers supported by dive-bombing aircraft to overpower their enemies.

	Occupied by Germany
	German allies
	At war with Germany
	Neutral

Norway

Sweden

Denmark

United Kingdom

Netherlands

Belgium

Germany

Russia

France

Slovakia

Switzerland

Hungary

Romania

Italy

Spain

German forces controlled most of Western Europe in June 1940.

The invasion plan was codenamed Operation Sealion. Germany planned to land 260,000 troops on the south coast of England in the first three days of the invasion. More tanks and troops would follow. They hoped to overwhelm the defending forces, just as they had done in France.

How to get these troops to England was the problem for the German navy. Britain's Royal Navy had more than five times as many ships as the Germans in 1940. The troops themselves would have to be carried on large slow-moving barges, which would be easy targets for attack by British aircraft.

Air power

The Luftwaffe needed to defeat the British Royal Air Force (RAF). If the Luftwaffe controlled the skies over the English Channel, its aircraft could combat the huge threat of the Royal Navy and help the invasion troops to reach England safely.

The Allied air force (which included pilots from Poland, Canada, France and many other countries as well as Britain) had fewer aircraft in July 1940 than the German Luftwaffe. But the defenders had advantages from fighting on home ground. If the Luftwaffe pilots were forced to land, they'd face capture in enemy territory.

The Battle of Britain was fought between June and October 1940. It was one of the first conflicts in which air power was so important. Small advances in aircraft design or technology could hold the key to victory.

The Royal Navy stood in the path of a German invasion.

Outnumbered

In early August 1940, Germany could call on many
more attacking aircraft than the Allied defenders.

- Luftwaffe aircraft:

    1,137 fighter aircraft

    949 bomber aircraft

    336 dive bombers

- Royal Air Force Fighter Command:

    1,032 fighter aircraft

Britain's factories were building more than 400 new
fighters every month.

Dogfight

The battle to control the skies above Britain was fought between fleets of fighter aircraft on both sides. The German air **offensive** against Britain was called Eagle Attack and it began on 13th August 1940. Germany launched waves of fighter and bomber aircraft to attack airfields and port cities in southern England. Allied fighter aircraft took off at a few minutes' notice to repel these attacks. The aerial battles between aircraft were called dogfights.

The secret of survival in a dogfight was to get into the sky quickly and swoop down to attack the enemy. After that, the pilot was desperate to get out of the area as quickly as possible before he came under attack himself. The speed and firepower of the aircraft could mean the difference between life and death, but which aircraft had the advantage?

People in southern England could see deadly dogfights in the sky above their homes.

Messerschmitt Bf 109

The Messerschmitt Bf 109 was the German aeroplane that RAF and Allied pilots feared the most.

It could climb and dive faster than any British fighter. It also had much more firepower than its rivals, with two cannons and two machine guns.

a Messerschmitt Bf 109 in action

The Bf 109 wasn't perfect though. It couldn't carry enough fuel to fly long distances. This was a big problem when German planes had to cross the English Channel. Also, the plane's powerful cannon only carried enough **ammunition** to fire about seven seconds.

Supermarine Spitfire

In 1934, Britain's Air Ministry asked Reginald Mitchell, an engineer with the Supermarine company, to design a fast, single-engined fighter. He created the Spitfire. This aircraft played a very important part in the Battle of Britain.

The Spitfire had a light and robust metal frame. The plane's design and its Rolls Royce Merlin engine enabled the Spitfire to fly faster than any other British aircraft. It could also turn more tightly than the Messerschmitt Bf 109. The Spitfire particularly outperformed the Messerschmitt at higher **altitude**.

When the call came to "**scramble**", or take off, pilots had to move fast.

Around 22,000 Spitfires were built during the war. Engineers were constantly improving them to keep one step ahead of the enemy.

Rear-view mirrors

Fighter pilots had to be constantly checking to see if an enemy aircraft was on their tail. Early models of the Spitfire didn't have rear-view mirrors so the pilots fitted car mirrors to their aircraft.

powerful Merlin engine to match the speed of Germany's fastest fighters

eight machine guns firing a combined 160 rounds per second

curved wing design for turning sharply

Why was the Spitfire so successful?

Hawker Hurricane

The Hurricane was the workhorse of the RAF. These aircraft were slower than the Spitfire or the Messerschmitt Bf 109, but they shot down more than 600 aircraft during the Battle of Britain.

The Hurricane's body was an old-fashioned design made from fabric stretched over a wood and metal frame. They could be repaired and back in the air quickly if they were damaged by enemy fire.

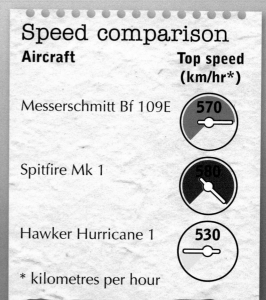

Speed comparison

Aircraft	Top speed (km/hr*)
Messerschmitt Bf 109E	570
Spitfire Mk 1	580
Hawker Hurricane 1	530

* kilometres per hour

The Hurricanes' main targets were slower-moving enemy bombers, where the fighters' lack of pace was less of a problem.

Easy targets

Pilots soon discovered the weaknesses of older aircraft, such as the British Boulton Paul Defiant. The Defiant was a two-seater aircraft with a separate **gun turret**. This slow fighter was an easy target for the Messerschmitt Bf 109s. The Luftwaffe had their own two-seater fighter, the Messerschmitt Bf 110, designed for long-range attacks. They weren't able to turn and dodge the attacks of Spitfires and Hurricanes.

A rear-view mirror above the cockpit was essential equipment for fighter pilots.

Learning lessons

Aircraft technology continued to develop week-by-week during the war, as each side tried to gain the upper hand. British engineers examined captured Messerschmitt aircraft. They desperately needed to discover how the planes could climb and dive so quickly. The secret lay in the Messerschmitt's propeller, which could be adjusted to give more power when climbing. The engineers used what they learnt to improve the British Spitfires and Hurricanes. Over 1,000 aircraft were converted to new propellers by mid-August 1940.

German pilots who crash-landed or parachuted to the ground were often captured.

The two sides' fighter aircraft were evenly matched, but the Allied pilots had the advantage that they were fighting close to home. If German pilots spent too long battling the RAF, they wouldn't have enough fuel for the return journey to France.

Aircraft technology was tested to the limit in the Battle of Britain. However, the aircraft were only as good as the pilots who flew them.

WOMEN OF BRITAIN

COME INTO THE FACTORIES

ASK AT ANY EMPLOYMENT EXCHANGE FOR ADVICE AND FULL DETAILS

This poster urged women to help save Britain by building more aircraft.

Air accidents

As much as 30% of aircraft damage and pilot injuries on both sides was caused by accidents rather than enemy fire. Fighter pilots were often inexperienced and exhausted by the constant life-or-death struggle in the skies.

Technology for pilots

For the pilots of the Battle of Britain, technology didn't just mean the aircraft they flew. They also relied on the equipment they carried, and the safety gear that might save their lives.

The biggest worry for commanders on both sides was that too many trained pilots would be killed or captured. The Allies lost 537 of around 3,000 aircrew during the Battle of Britain, but five times as many Luftwaffe pilots were killed or wounded.

Pilots would train on older aircraft with two sets of controls for the new pilot and his trainer, such as the de Havilland Tiger Moth biplane. Once they could fly solo, pilots were sent to their unit, called a **squadron**. Often, pilots had very little experience of flying single-seater aircraft before they took off into combat.

a de Havilland Tiger Moth
training aircraft

There were no computerised flying aids in a Spitfire or Hurricane. The pilot aimed his machine guns using a simple sighting device. With the target in his sight, the pilot pressed the gun button. Allied fighter planes only carried enough bullets to fire for 15 seconds so they couldn't afford to miss.

reflector sight

a cramped Spitfire cockpit, with the pilot's reflector sight in the centre

Clothing and equipment

In 1940, fighter planes could fly faster and higher than ever before, where the air is much colder. The pilots' clothing and safety equipment hadn't developed as fast as their aircraft. RAF pilots usually wore a standard woollen uniform, shirt and even a tie. Bulky flying jackets and trousers were too uncomfortable to wear in the hot summer of 1940.

Once the call to scramble came, there was no time to change anyway. Leather flying helmets included oxygen masks, and earpieces and microphones for communicating by radio. Silk scarves stopped pilots' necks rubbing on the RAF's rough uniforms as they constantly turned their heads looking for enemy fighters.

A pilot's greatest fear was a direct hit in the fuel tank at the front of the aircraft. The pilot would have to open his cockpit hood and turn the aircraft upside down to get out, relying on his parachute for

Each pilot had a parachute and life jacket.

a safe landing. There were no ejector seats to release them safely from a doomed aircraft. Late in 1940, a device was added to release the cockpit canopy more quickly.

goggles

leather
flying helmet
including
radio headset

Full flying gear
gave protection
from the cold but
could be too bulky
to wear when pilots
were racing to
take off and meet
enemy attacks.

life jacket

insulated
flying jacket
and trousers

Fluorescein

Fluorescent dye was
released if a pilot landed
in the sea. The bright
patch of water would
guide rescuers to
the missing airman.

fur-lined boots

Bombing raids

The Battle of Britain is famous for battles between brave pilots in their Spitfire and Messerschmitt fighter planes, but bombers also played a key part in the battle. Germany wanted to control the skies, and to do this they had to destroy airfields, aircraft on the ground, and the factories where they were made.

In July 1940, the Luftwaffe's forces in northern France included more than 1,000 bomber aircraft, ranging from the ageing Heinkels to the terrifying Junkers Ju87 dive bombers.

A German Stuka dives to attack.

This Heinkel 111 crashed before it could reach its target.

Heinkel 111 and Dornier 17 bombers were quite old by 1940. They were slow and had little firepower to repel attack by Allied Spitfires and Hurricanes. Each aircraft could only carry around 1,000 kilograms of bombs, which was much less than the bombers used later in the war.

The Junkers Ju87 was known as the Stuka, a shortened version of the German word for dive bomber. These aircraft had been at the centre of the German Blitzkrieg against France, diving towards Allied troops with a terrifying wail and releasing their bombs with deadly accuracy.

The Stuka had great success attacking troops on the ground and ships at sea, but the slow, lumbering dive bomber was outgunned by fast-moving fighters in the Battle of Britain. On 18th August, 12 Stukas were destroyed in a single raid and others were badly damaged.

The Junkers 88 could fly further and carried more bombs than the Luftwaffe's other bombers, but it was still too slow to outrun the Allied fighters. These bombers had to be protected by Messerschmitt Bf 109s, which meant that Germany's best aircraft weren't able to focus on attacking the RAF's Spitfires and Hurricanes.

German attacks on airfields created problems for Fighter Command.

Cities under attack

In July 1940, the Luftwaffe's bombers attacked Britain's ports, shipping and military bases. In August, they switched to attacking the Allied air force, including aircraft factories and airfields.

All citizens could be targets for the bombers and thousands more people died from air raids than were killed in the aerial battles of 1940. There were also fears that German bombers would attack using poison gas, but gas wasn't used against Britain.

a gas mask

All citizens had to carry gas masks at all times in case of attack by poison gas.

Defensive technology

By July 1940, Britain's anti-aircraft defences on the ground included 1,204 heavy and 581 light anti-aircraft guns, which protected aircraft factories, airfields and ports. This was well short of what was needed to deal with the threat from hundreds of bombers.

The anti-aircraft crews received a warning by phone when enemy aircraft were approaching. Air-raid sirens would sound and people would drop everything to rush to the air-raid shelters. Large tethered balloons called barrage balloons were launched to protect important sites, and some were even attached to ships. The balloons forced enemy planes to fly higher which meant that they were less accurate with their firing.

Enemy pilots risked being caught in the wires that tied the balloons to the ground.

Confusing the bombers

The British government set up a top-secret department to deceive German bombers and hide key targets. Many of those who worked on these **decoys** had worked in the film industry before the war. They created dummy airfields, including dummy aircraft, buildings and night-time lights. Elsewhere, they used lights and fire to imitate a burning city at night. They hoped German bombers would attack these rather than their real targets.

Searchlights were used to pick out enemy aircraft at night.

Command and control

The nerve centre of Britain's air defences was the Fighter Command Headquarters. Information about enemy fighters and bombing raids flooded into this bustling but efficient control centre. Fighter Command could then direct Spitfires and Hurricanes to be scrambled and tackle the danger.

Information about enemy attacks came from the **radar** system around the coast. Fighter Command also had a network of 30,000 observers across the country who'd phone in eyewitness reports of enemy aircraft.

Once an attack was under way, it would be plotted on a large map table. Plotters received instructions through telephone headsets. They used coloured counters to show the number, height and type of enemy aircraft that had been spotted.

Each five-minute section of this clock has a different colour. These colours were used to show when aircraft movements were updated on the plotter table.

Commanders would stand on a platform so they could see the whole table. Today, they'd use computer screens, but the plotter table ensured that everyone knew the latest situation across the country.

Plotters were members of the Women's Auxiliary Air Force (WAAF).

Smaller group headquarters around the country used the same system as Fighter Command's central control room. A board with a series of coloured lights showed whether each squadron of Allied aircraft was ready for action, already in the air or just landing and refuelling. This information was essential to ensure they met the threat in time.

Goering's plan

Luftwaffe chief Hermann Goering chose to direct the air attack from his castle near Berlin. German **intelligence** was poor and Goering knew little about Dowding's control system.

He expected his pilots to overwhelm the RAF in a few days. Dowding's organised defence system ensured that didn't happen. German pilots soon discovered that, wherever they attacked, the RAF was there before them.

If RAF fighters were scrambled quickly enough they could fly higher than the German aircraft. This could be a decisive advantage in a dogfight.

Hugh Dowding

Air Chief Marshal Dowding was the head of Fighter Command and in charge of Britain's fighter squadrons. He knew that technology had a vital part to play in Britain's defence. Radar, radio and telephone communication were very important parts of the command and control system he introduced.

Air Chief Marshal Dowding

Radar

Dowding's command system relied on early warning about German raids. New radar technology made it possible, for the first time, to detect aircraft before they could actually be seen.

Robert Watson-Watt, scientist and inventor

Experiments with radar had begun during the 1930s, when scientists investigated how the armed forces could use **radio waves**. British military chiefs were concerned that Germany could develop a "death ray" weapon. Although the scientists concluded this wasn't possible, Robert Watson-Watt suggested radio waves could be used to detect enemy aircraft.

Watson-Watt started experimenting to prove that radio waves from a transmitter would bounce off a solid object, such as an aircraft. The system would automatically measure how long the radio waves took to bounce back – this would show how far away the aircraft was.

When war broke out in 1939, 21 radar stations with masts up to 110 metres high had been built around Britain's coasts. There was also a series of stations with lower masts. This network was called Chain Home.

Together, they could detect enemy aircraft taking off 190 kilometres away. The radar system could tell the size of a raid, the direction it was travelling and its altitude.

Chain Home radar towers

Radar benefits and drawbacks

With the help of radar, Fighter Command knew when enemy planes had taken off and where they were heading. Fighter aircraft could be scrambled to meet the threat. Without radar, Allied pilots would have had to spend much more time in the air looking out for German raids. They saved fuel and also had more time for much-needed rest.

Britain's radar system wasn't perfect. It could only detect aircraft coming across the sea as the transmitters faced in that direction. Once the enemy had flown over the coast, they were invisible to radar.

The Chain Home radar stations were also very easy to spot. On 11th August 1940, German bombers attacked Chain Home. They believed they'd badly damaged several stations with huge bombs, but most of the stations were operating again in a few hours. Germany's commanders decided to focus on destroying aircraft rather than radar. This was a big mistake.

A radar operator studies her screen for any sign of enemy aircraft.

German radar

Germany had developed a different radar system of its own. The German navy carried radar equipment to find the position of enemy ships.

"Würzburg" mobile radar units could be located wherever they were needed on land, unlike Britain's giant Chain Home stations. The mobile units only worked over a very short range but they could track enemy aircraft in the area around an anti-aircraft gun. They rotated rather than pointing in one direction.

The Chain Home system that defended Britain in 1940 was less advanced than German radar, but British forces got the most out of their radar technology. Whenever German planes reached England, the RAF's fighters were there to meet them.

a German mobile radar system

Fooling the radar

Both sides thought of dropping clouds of metal strips like tin foil from planes to confuse the radar systems into mistaking the foil for aircraft. They were reluctant to try it. They were worried that their enemies would use the same method, and make their own radar defences useless.

Radio and communication

Fighter Command's control system and radar gathered information about enemy attacks, but this had to be communicated to the pilots, on the ground or in midair. For this, they needed the latest radio technology.

With radio communication, pilots could be directed towards enemy attacks even once they were in the air. RAF pilots could use their radios to communicate directly back to their bases via radio receivers on the ground.

Radio operators also played an important role in listening to enemy messages.

Fighter Command introduced a system of code words to make communication easier. When the order came to "scramble", the squadron had to take off as soon as possible to deal with "bandits", meaning enemy aircraft. The word "vector" was used to tell pilots which direction they needed to fly in.

The Luftwaffe pilots attacking Britain could talk to other pilots in their unit by radio, but there was no ground-to-air communication. Germany had the right equipment, but many pilots thought that carrying a radio was a waste of time. Once they took off for their mission, these pilots were on their own.

German fighter pilots could communicate directly with other fighter pilots, but not with the bomber crews they escorted.

Locating friend and foe

The RAF's Pip-Squeak system used radio to pinpoint the location of squadrons in the air. Regular radio transmissions from aircraft were picked up by the antennae on the ground. The system told Allied controllers the exact position of their aircraft in the sky. Pip-Squeak was essential for mapping the battle over England as British radar could only detect aircraft before they reached the coast.

The Luftwaffe used radio technology for navigation and locating targets for bombing. Two beams of radio waves were transmitted from Europe. Pilots followed one of the beams and dropped their bombs where the two beams crossed.

"........ but for Heaven's sake don't say I told you!"

CARELESS TALK COSTS LIVES

Posters reminded everyone how important secrecy was.

British intelligence uncovered this "Knickebein", or "Crooked Leg" system. They set out to disrupt the beams with radio waves of their own.

Secure messages

In 1940, telephone calls were all carried by wires. Government and military leaders were well aware that enemy spies could listen into telephone calls. Scrambler units were fitted to phones used for sensitive information, such as directing air defences.

In the government's underground headquarters, scrambler phones were used to give orders to military forces across Britain.

Defending Britain's coast

Commanders on both sides knew that the battle raging in the skies was just the first part of Germany's invasion plan. Engineers also had to find new ways of defending Britain against attacks from the sea.

Britain's south coast was lined with coils of barbed wire, which would slow down any troops landing on the beaches. Concrete **pillboxes** were built as guard posts across the country.

The Petroleum Warfare Department in Britain laid pipes beneath the sea and along major roads. They'd release burning oil so that an invading force would be met with a wall of fire. Low-flying aircraft could be targeted by vertical flame-throwers.

Forts were built on towers in the North Sea as a first line of defence.

40

Mine menace

The coast of Britain was surrounded by explosive **mines**, laid by both sides. Mines were fixed in place by a weight, which sat on the seabed and held the mine a few feet below the surface. If a ship hit the mine, the huge explosive could sink it in a few minutes. British mine-sweeping boats towed a cable to cut the lines securing the mines underwater. They were exploded when they bobbed up to the surface.

Disarming a mine was dangerous work.

Codebreakers

In wartime, information about the enemy's forces and plans could mean the difference between victory and defeat. Gathering intelligence through spies was unreliable, especially as many of them were actually working for the other side. Teams of codebreakers used new technology to stay one step ahead by gathering and decoding secret enemy communications.

Three-quarters of the 10,000 codebreakers who worked at Bletchley Park were women.

Intelligence on both sides was gathered by listening in to radio and telephone messages. This was relatively easy if the signals weren't encoded, such as radio conversations between pilots. However, Allied intelligence services needed to be constantly alert. There was no way of recording all the radio messages and there was always the danger of missing a message that could cost or save thousands of lives.

Many of the messages seemed to be random strings of letters transmitted as a series of dots and dashes. These messages had to be copied down with total accuracy to be decoded by the Government Code and Cipher School at Bletchley Park, Buckinghamshire.

Some of Britain's finest minds worked to crack enemy codes at Bletchley Park.

Enigma

The most secret German messages were sent using an Enigma machine. The Germans believed the Enigma code was unbreakable, but the Allies were determined to solve the puzzle. Today, a computer would be able to check all the possible combinations of letters. Back in 1940, the codebreakers at Bletchley Park had to invent a new machine to crack the code.

The Enigma code was broken for the first time in January 1940 and a large team of codebreakers worked to decipher messages as the code changed. This was made much quicker and easier with the invention of a machine called the Bombe by mathematicians Alan Turing and Gordon Welchman.

Alan Turing

Decoded Enigma messages were top secret and only a few people were allowed to see them. Fighter Command had a direct link to Bletchley Park and used these messages to plan the defence of Britain. But they had to be careful. If Germany discovered that Enigma had been cracked, they would have stopped using it.

Operators typed a message into the Enigma machine, which would then be scrambled through a series of wires and wheels to create a coded message.

Winning the battle

On the first day of the Luftwaffe's air attacks against Britain, they used 485 bombers and 1,000 fighter aircraft. Ferocious attacks like this continued for three weeks. In most attacks, the Luftwaffe lost more aircraft than the Allies. German intelligence said that the RAF was close to defeat, but they were wrong. In fact, Britain's aircraft factories were producing more aircraft than the Luftwaffe could shoot down.

Britain's factories produced more than 2,000 Spitfires and Hurricanes between June and October 1940.

But Fighter Command's leader, Hugh Dowding, still had two big problems. The first was the damage being done to airfields by German bombers. The RAF now had fewer bases to operate from. He was also worried about the number of pilots being killed and wounded. It took months to train their replacements. The constant attacks had left all of Fighter Command's pilots exhausted. How much longer could they defend Britain?

Lack of rest was one of the main dangers for fighter pilots in August 1940.

Change of tactics

On 7th September 1940, as things were getting desperate, the Luftwaffe suddenly changed tactics. More than 1,000 aircraft crossed the English Channel and battled the RAF in the skies above southeast England. But this bombing raid wasn't aimed at the damaged airfields. Most of the bombs were dropped on the docks of East London, which were an important centre for British industry.

While the people of London suffered, the RAF had time to recover. On 19th September 1940, Hitler cancelled plans to invade Britain. Attacks continued into October, but the Luftwaffe had failed in its mission to destroy Britain's air defences.

During the Blitz in 1940 and 1941, Germany launched nightly raids on British cities.

Prime Minister Churchill spent much of his time in this underground bunker. The bunker used technological innovations such as lights that imitated daylight, and air pumped in from outside.

Battle-winning technology

The Battle of Britain couldn't have been won without the courage and skill of the RAF's pilots, from Britain and many other countries. But the battle would have been lost without the Spitfire, which could match the Luftwaffe's best aircraft. Luftwaffe raids also failed to destroy Britain's essential radar system.

Shaping the modern world

By October 1940, Britain was safe from German invasion.
But bombs still rained down on London and other cities.

In 1941, the tide of war started to turn against Hitler.
The **Soviet Union** and the USA joined Great Britain in
an alliance against Germany and her allies, including Japan.
Germany and Japan surrendered in 1945.

Just as scientists and engineers had helped to win the Battle of
Britain, both sides continued to look for inventions that would
win them the war. Many of their inventions shaped the world we
live in today.

Jet engines

Jet engines were invented separately
by Briton Frank Whittle and
German engineers. The first jet
fighters appeared in 1944.

Britain's first jet
aircraft was tested
in 1941.

the Colossus computer

Penicillin

The first antibiotic medicine to cure infections was discovered by Alexander Fleming in 1928. It became available for medical use in 1941.

Nuclear power

The first atomic bombs killed tens of thousands of people in Japan's cities. The same technology was used to develop nuclear power stations.

Computers

Colossus, the first electronic programmable computer, was used at Bletchley Park from 1944 to break enemy codes. This invention remained top secret until 1975.

Space travel

The first rocket to travel to the edge of space was the German V2. More than 1,300 V2 rocket missiles were fired at Britain in 1944 and 1945.

Glossary

Allies	countries fighting against Germany in World War Two
altitude	how high above the ground, or sea level, something is
ammunition	bullets and explosives required for guns and other weapons
Blitzkrieg	German word meaning "lightning war" and referring to the way Germany's forces used tanks and infantry supported by aircraft in World War Two
decoys	things designed to deceive an enemy
evacuate	move someone from a dangerous place, such as a city being attacked, to a safer place
gun turret	a small tower on an aircraft housing one or more guns
intelligence	information gathered during wartime, for example, by spies or listening to enemy communications
mines	hidden bombs designed to explode when they are touched, for example, by a ship at sea
offensive	military attack
pillboxes	small concrete shelters used as guard posts
radar	(radio direction and ranging) device that uses radio waves to detect objects such as aircraft
radio waves	type of radiation used to communicate or transmit TV and radio programmes over long distances
scramble	code word instructing aircraft to take off immediately during Battle of Britain
squadron	section of an air force made up of a number of aircraft, their pilots and crews
Soviet Union	former country made up of what are now Russia, Ukraine and other countries
tactics	methods or plans for doing something, including fighting a battle

Index

Gaining an advantage

Technology	Britain
fighter aircraft	The Spitfire turned more tightly and faster at high altitude.
command structure	Command system gathered intelligence and directed aircraft where they were needed.
radar	Radar gave early warning of enemy attacks, saving time and fuel.
radio and communication	Ground-to-air radio and Pip-Squeak system were important parts of command system.
intelligence	Intelligence services and Government Code and Cipher School were able to crack most secret enemy codes.

Germany

equally balanced →	Messerschmitt Bf 109 could climb and dive faster than rivals, with more firepower.
advantage to Britain	Poor intelligence and planning mistakes reduced impact of attacks.
advantage to Britain	Failed to destroy Chain Home radar or realise how important it was to British defence.
advantage to Britain	Made less use of radio communication. Crooked Leg system used to locate targets.
advantage to Britain	There was a lack of correct intelligence about RAF strength during Battle of Britain.

Ideas for reading

Written by Clare Dowdall, PhD
Lecturer and Primary Literacy Consultant

Reading objectives:
- make comparisons within and across books
- discuss their understanding
- ask questions to improve their understanding
- summarise the main ideas drawn from more than one paragraph, identifying key details that support the main ideas

Spoken language objectives:
- ask relevant questions to extend their understanding and knowledge

Curriculum links: History – British history

Resources: ICT for research, papers and pencils/pens for mind-mapping, art materials for advertisements.

Build a context for reading
- Ask children to share what they know about the Battle of Britain and collect any ideas as a mind map.
- Hand out the books and look at the covers. Ask children to define the word *technology*, and relate their understanding to familiar examples.
- Read the blurb together. Ask questions to build a context for their reading. Establish that this is a battle of World War Two. Check that they know what the acronym RAF stands for, and can read *Luftwaffe*. Discuss what is shown in the pictures.

- ## Understand and apply reading strategies
- Read pp2–3 together. Based on their reading, discuss children's understanding of World War Two and why the Battle of Britain would be such an important event. Challenge children to suggest why future generations would remember the Battle of Britain as "their finest hour".